SCIENCE Q&A

PHYSICAL SCIENCE

Cavendish
Square
New York

Published in 2016 by Cavendish Square Publishing, LLC
243 5th Avenue, Suite 136, New York, NY 10016

© 2016 Brown Bear Books Ltd

First Edition

Website: cavendishsq.com

CPSIA Compliance Information: Batch #WS15CSQ

Library of Congress Cataloging-in-Publication Data

Physical science / edited by Tim Harris.
p. cm. — (Science Q&A)
Includes index.
ISBN 978-1-50260-625-9 (hardcover) ISBN 978-1-50260-624-2 (paperback)
ISBN 978-1-50260-626-6 (ebook)
1. Physical sciences — Juvenile literature. I. Harris, Tim. II. Title.

Q163.H37 2015
530—d23

For Brown Bear Books Ltd:
Editors: Tracey Kelly, Dawn Titmus, Tim Harris
Designer: Mary Walsh
Design Manager: Keith Davis
Editorial Director: Lindsey Lowe
Children's Publisher: Anne O'Daly
Picture Manager: Sophie Mortimer

Picture Credits:
T=Top, C=Center, B=Bottom, L=Left, R=Right

Front Cover : All pictures Shutterstock/Thinkstock.
Inside: Alamy: Paul Risdale 23tl; Corbis: Patrick Giadorno 14tr; iStockphoto: 19bl; Shutterstock: 11tl, 11bc, 22tl, Alphaspirit 4, 10tl, Darryl Brooks 26cr, Gregory Fer 10b, Ivan Kuzmin 19tr, Joyce Michaud 15tr, Pedro Saaverria 6bl, Vasyl Yakobchuk 27br, Zoonar 6cr; Thinkstock: Comstock 1, 7t, 27tc, iStockphoto 5tl, 11tr, 14tl.

Brown Bear Books has made every attempt to contact the copyright holder.
If you have any information please contact licensing@brownbearbooks.co.uk

Printed in the United States of America

CONTENTS

INTRODUCTION

The study of nonliving things is called physical science. From things we can see, such as a rock or a car, to energy we cannot see, such as sound, electricity, and heat, physical science explores how nonliving things are made and how they work.

Everything in the world around us is made up of matter and chemicals, and all matter is made up of elements—tiny particles called atoms. You will find out about the different states of matter—solid, liquid, and gas—such as when you drop an ice cube from your glass on a hot summer's day and watch it melt into water, then evaporate into steam on the sidewalk. You will also discover what happens when two or more elements bond together to form a molecule, and how chemical reactions take place, such as when a detergent washes your clothes. You will learn about different materials, such as diamonds, which are very hard, and more flexible ones, such as the rubber used in a car tire.

◄ Diamond is the hardest naturally occurring material on Earth. It is made of a crystalline form of pure carbon.

When a tennis player hits a ball with a racket, he or she is using a push force to propel the ball into the air toward the opponent's court.

Organic materials come from things that were once-living plants or animals, and synthetic materials are made from chemicals that do not occur naturally, such as plastics. Find out what household items are made from and what properties make them perfect for each use.

When you hear a song, do you wonder how the music reaches your ears? Sound is a form of energy that travels in waves through air, water, and even metal. Light also travels in waves and is made up of electric and magnetic energy. There are other forms of energy, too: heat, mechanical, electrical, nuclear, and chemical.

What keeps us on Earth, not flying off into space? What keeps an airplane flying? Forces such as gravity, thrust, lift, and drag change an object's speed and direction. It is gravity that keeps our feet planted firmly on the ground.

▶ Some molecules are simple and others are complex, such as this model. The balls represent atoms and the bars are their links.

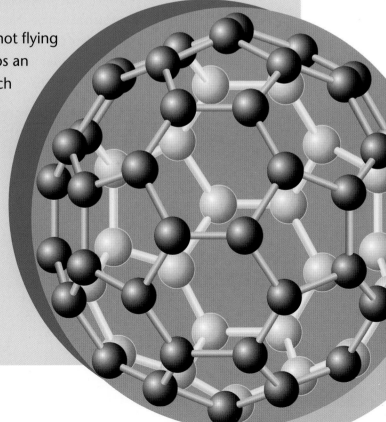

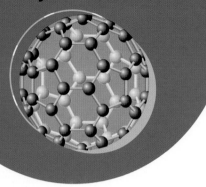

CHEMICALS AND MATTER

Everything around us is made of chemicals and matter. And all the matter exists in one of three forms: as a liquid, a solid, or a gas.

▼ The Guggenheim Museum in Bilbao, Spain, is a spectacular building. The shiny effect is created by panels of the metal element titanium (symbol Ti).

Matter can change from one form to another, such as when solid ice cream melts and becomes liquid. All matter is made of elements. An element cannot be reduced to a simpler substance. And all elements are made of tiny particles called atoms. Each element has a symbol of one or two letters. For instance, chemists write oxygen as O, iron as Fe, and aluminum as Al.

Different Elements

When two or more atoms join together, they form a molecule. A substance can be made of molecules of the same element or of lots of different elements. For example, a gold bar is made of the

▲ Plants grow when carbon dioxide and water react to form sugar. This is called photosynthesis.

metallic element gold (chemical symbol Au) and nothing else. A brass object, however, is a mixture of copper (Cu) and zinc (Zn).

Atoms and molecules combine in different ways to form solids, liquids,

CATALYSTS
Chemists have to be able to control which reactions happen and how quickly they happen. They use catalysts to do this. Catalysts are substances that control the rate of a chemical reaction while not being changed themselves.

▲ Fireworks explode when heat is added to a mixture of chemicals, which burn in different colors.

and gases. These three types are called states of matter. For instance, water is made up of two elements, hydrogen (H) and oxygen (O), whose atoms join to form water molecules. Water can exist as a solid (ice), a liquid (water), and a gas (steam).

States of Matter

Solids have a definite shape and volume. Liquids have a definite volume, but not a definite shape. A liquid takes the shape of the container it is poured into. Gases change their shape and volume. They spread out to fill any container they are put in and can easily be squeezed into a smaller space, unlike a liquid or a solid.

Chemical Reactions

A chemical reaction is any process that changes one chemical into another. Some examples of chemical reactions include the human body turning food into energy, iron becoming rusty, and fireworks exploding in the night sky. Thousands of reactions are taking place all the time. Some look dramatic, but we do not even notice that others are taking place.

STATES OF MATTER

Molecules in a solid are packed closely together in a regular pattern

Molecules in a liquid are fairly close but not in a regular pattern

Molecules in a gas are well spread, with no regular pattern

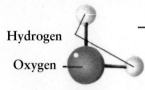

Hydrogen

Oxygen

Water molecule

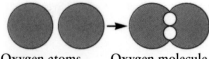

Oxygen atoms   Oxygen molecule

Q What are molecules?

A A molecule (above) is the simplest part of a substance that can take part in chemical reactions. It is a group of two or more atoms linked together. The atoms may be the same or different. For example, a molecule of water is made of two hydrogen atoms linked to an oxygen atom. An oxygen molecule is made of two oxygen atoms linked together.

Q What is the difference between a mixture and a compound?

A If iron filings and sulfur (1) are mixed together (2), there is no chemical reaction, and they can be separated again by removing the iron with a magnet (3). When iron filings and sulfur are heated (4), they combine and change into iron sulfide, a compound.

1   2

3   4

Q What chemicals are used in fire extinguishers?

A Carbon dioxide extinguishers send out a jet of carbon dioxide gas. Dry powder extinguishers blanket a fire with powder. Soda-acid extinguishers (right) mix sulfuric acid with sodium carbonate, making carbon dioxide gas, which forces out a jet of water.

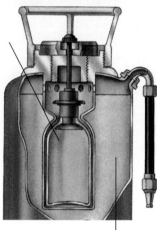

Sulfuric acid

Sodium carbonate

Q How do soaps and detergents work?

A Soaps and detergents are made from long molecules that are water-loving at one end and grease-loving at the other end. When they go to work on a dirty cloth, they surround each droplet of greasy dirt stuck to the fibers of the cloth with their grease-loving tails plugged into the grease droplet (below). The coated droplet then floats off the cloth into the water and is washed away.

Grease

Cloth

Q How are chemicals made?

A The chemical industry makes chemicals by processing raw materials with heat, pressure, and chemical reactions. Sulfuric acid is made from sulfur in a series of stages (right) that change sulfur into different compounds, ending with sulfuric acid.

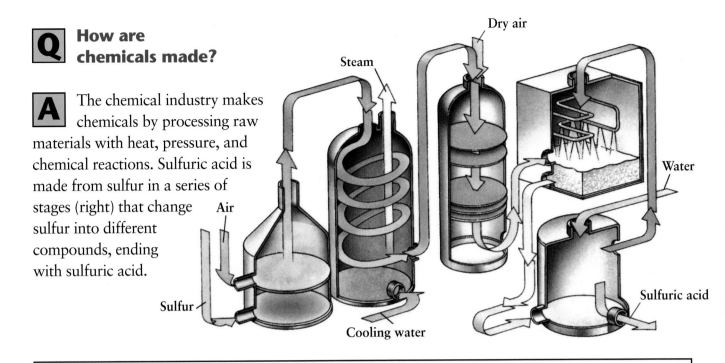

Dry air

Steam

Air

Water

Sulfur

Cooling water

Sulfuric acid

Q What are crystals?

A Crystals are solid pieces of material with flat faces set at angles to each other. All crystals of the same substance have the same angles between their faces. Crystals form in this way because their atoms always lie in the same regular patterns. Salt, sugar, and quartz are crystals. Minerals can sometimes be identified by the shape of their crystals.

Q What is chemical analysis?

A Chemists use chemical analysis (right) to find out what an unknown substance contains. There are several methods. Volumetric analysis involves reactions in solutions. Gravimetric analysis involves weighing. In gas-liquid chromatography, gas carries the sample through a column of moist powder. The sample separates into simpler compounds, which are recorded on a chart as they leave the column.

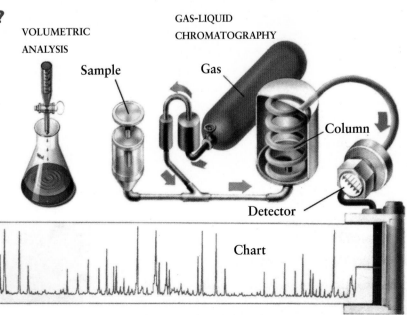

VOLUMETRIC ANALYSIS

GAS-LIQUID CHROMATOGRAPHY

Sample

Gas

Column

Detector

Chart

MATERIALS

Everything—from houses and clothing to cars, computers, and footballs—is made of materials. Different materials are suited to different jobs.

In nature, some materials are hard and others are soft. Some are heavy and others are light. When choosing the material to make something, a designer has to decide what is most suitable. So, a car tire has to be flexible to give the passengers a smooth ride but tough so as not to burst easily. The supports for a tall building have to be strong enough to support enormous weights. A yacht's sides need to be both strong and light, so that waves do not crush the vessel and it does not sit too low in the water. A child's plush toy needs to be soft and light.

Metallic Materials

The simplest materials are those made of just one element. A gold bar is made of the metallic element gold and nothing else.

Alloys are another type of metallic material. They are a mixture of two or more different elements.

▼ Diamonds are a very hard material because of the special arrangement of their carbon atoms.

▲ A gold bar is heavy, very valuable, and made of just the element gold (Au).

Steel is an example of an alloy. It is composed mostly of iron, but it is stronger than iron. Steel also contains elements such as carbon, manganese, and nickel.

Brass is another alloy. It is a shiny yellowish metal, which is often used for decoration. Brass is a mixture of copper and zinc. Bronze is an alloy that is made of copper and tin. And nickel coins are made of copper and nickel.

Ceramics

Ceramics are different again. Cups and plates are examples of ceramics. The main chemicals used in ceramics are minerals found in the natural world, such as quartz (silicon dioxide, SiO_2), periclase (magnesium oxide, MgO), and hematite (ferric oxide, Fe_2O_3). When ceramics are manufactured, these materials have to be heated to a great temperature and then cooled again. Glass is a particular kind of ceramic material that is often transparent, and so it is ideal for making windows.

Plastics

Plastics are usually made from chemicals that do not occur naturally. They are called synthetics and have to be made by chemists, usually from the products of oil. Plastics can be molded into every possible shape. Some are bendable and others are sturdier, and most are tough. Televisions, computers,

▲ Many canoes are made from fiberglass, which is a strong and light material.

game consoles, cars, and cell phones all have parts made of plastic components. Composite materials contain two or more different kinds of materials. The hull of a boat, for instance, may be made of fiberglass, which is both strong and light. Fiberglass has fine fibers of glass embedded in a plastic material. Car brake pads are made of a soft metal with hard ceramic particles mixed in.

ORGANIC MATERIALS
Organic materials come from living or once-living plants or animals. So wood comes from trees, and coal and oil come from the fossilized remains of plants and tiny animals. Natural rubber comes from the milky secretions (latex) of the rubber tree, *Hevea brasiliensis*. The latex is allowed to dry, then ground and dissolved in a solvent. Other chemicals are then added to stiffen or color the rubber.

GENERAL INFORMATION
- The hardness of a material is measured with the Mohs scale. It ranges from 1 (soft) to 10 (hard).
- There are many types of plastics, including polyethylene, which is used to make plastic bags and plastic wrap.

Metal fuselage

Q What are materials?

A Materials are what we use to make the things we need. The first people used natural materials such as rock, wood, plant fibers, and animal bones and skins. Then they learned how to make new materials. They made clay pots and baked them at high temperatures to harden them. They discovered how to make iron, bronze, copper, and other metals. Glass was being made as far back as five thousand years ago. Today, we use more materials than ever, including a wide range of plastics.

Rubber tires

Pottery vase

Glass flask

Plastic pen

Wood

Q What materials come from plants?

A People have used materials taken from plants since prehistoric times, and plants are still a very important source of materials today. Timber, resins, rubber, cotton, linen, dyes, essential oils, and a wide range of medicines are still obtained from plants.

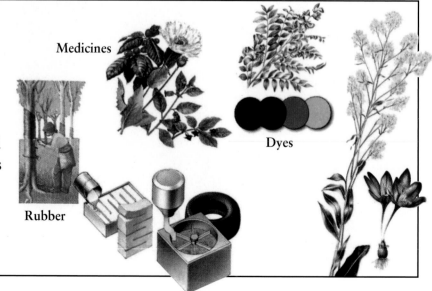

Medicines

Dyes

Rubber

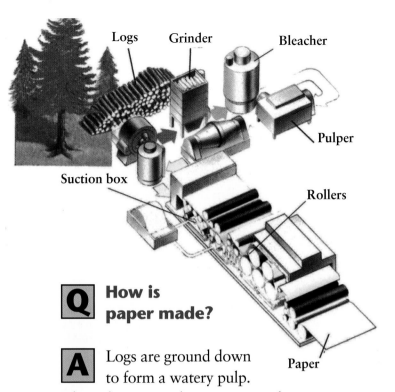

Logs Grinder Bleacher

Pulper

Suction box

Rollers

Q How is paper made?

Paper

A Logs are ground down to form a watery pulp. The pulp is poured onto wire mesh. Water is sucked and rolled out, leaving a thin film of paper. The process is continuous. Pulp is fed into one end of the machine (above), and paper comes out at the other end.

Q What are composites?

A Composites are materials made by combining two or more materials. Many kinds of boats (above) are made by laying mats of glass fibers into a mold and then soaking the mats in liquid plastic. The plastic sets hard and is reinforced by the fibers to make a smooth, tough, lightweight hull.

Q What do we get from crude oil?

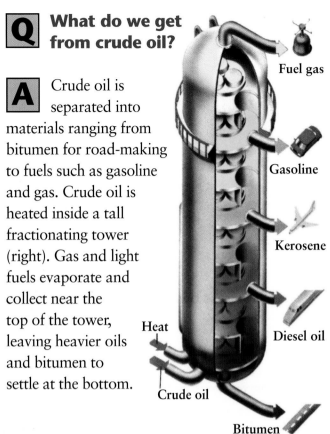

Fuel gas

Gasoline

Kerosene

Heat

Diesel oil

Crude oil

Bitumen

A Crude oil is separated into materials ranging from bitumen for road-making to fuels such as gasoline and gas. Crude oil is heated inside a tall fractionating tower (right). Gas and light fuels evaporate and collect near the top of the tower, leaving heavier oils and bitumen to settle at the bottom.

Q How is plastic recycled?

A Waste plastic is put into a furnace (below) and heated. The gas given off is then separated in a distillation column. Wax and tar collect at the bottom, while lighter gases collect farther up. Some of the gas is fed back to fuel the furnace, and some is used in industry.

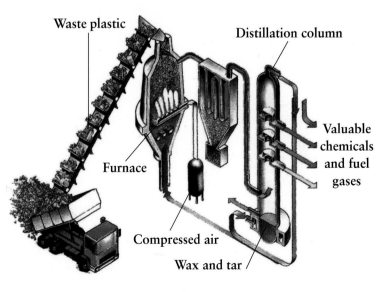

Waste plastic

Distillation column

Furnace

Valuable chemicals and fuel gases

Compressed air

Wax and tar

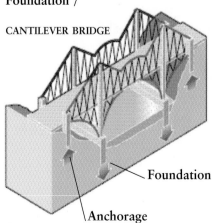

FORCES AND ENERGY

Force is a push or pull on an object. A force moves a stationary object or changes the direction or speed of a moving one. Energy makes things happen. There are several kinds of energy.

KEY FACTS

Unit of force: Newton (N). This is the amount of force needed to accelerate an object with a mass of 1 kg (2.2 pounds) by 1 meter (3.2 feet) per second, every second.

Unit of energy: Joule (J). This is the amount of energy need to apply a force of 1 newton over a distance of 1 meter (3.2 feet).

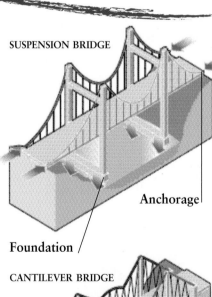

SUSPENSION BRIDGE

Anchorage

Foundation

CANTILEVER BRIDGE

Foundation

Anchorage

▲ Two hurdlers running at the same speed but in opposite directions. Their velocities are different because velocity is a combination of speed and direction.

Forces can make things slow down, speed up, or change direction. All these changes involve energy. For instance, a bullet in a gun is not moving, but when an explosive charge is detonated, it will apply a powerful force to the bullet. It will get faster (accelerate) very quickly and fly out of the gun barrel. When the bullet hits a wall, another force will act on the bullet and slow it to a complete stop.

Moving objects have kinetic energy. For example, waterwheels use the kinetic energy of moving water to perform mechanical tasks. A moving waterwheel is producing mechanical energy.

A ball balanced on a wall has potential energy, or the energy of position. When someone pushes the ball and it falls toward the ground, its potential energy is converted to kinetic energy.

A can of gasoline has latent energy. The gas is not doing any work, but if it is put in a car, and the

◄ The red arrows show where forces act as each bridge pushes down onto its foundations and pulls at its anchors on land.

CIRCULAR MOTION

When people spin around a swing carousel ride at a fair, their direction of motion is changing all the time. So they are constantly accelerating, even though their speed may not change at all. Forces that cause circular motion are called torques. They pull objects around a central point. If the torque force stops acting on the object, it will fly off in a straight line.

engine is started, it will start doing work—driving the engine. The burning gasoline in the car is producing heat energy.

Other Types of Energy

There are other types of energy, apart from mechanical and heat energy. They include electrical, chemical, sound, light, and nuclear energy. Electrical energy is the energy produced by an electric current to light a bulb, for instance. When the bulb lights up, the electrical energy changes to heat and light energy. Likewise, when its strings are picked or strummed, an electric guitar converts electrical energy to sound energy.

Energy Conservation

When one type of energy is converted to another—for instance, when electrical energy changes to heat and light in a light bulb—the total amount of energy stays the same. This is called the law of conservation of energy.

GENERAL INFORMATION

- The unit of force, the newton, is named after pioneering English scientist Isaac Newton (1642–1727).
- Newton explained that any object moving in a straight line continues to move in a straight line unless a force acts on it.
- The unit of energy, the joule, is named after English physicist James Prescott Joule (1818–1889).

▼ The different forces that can be applied to a ruler.

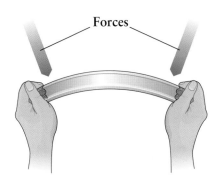

BENDING

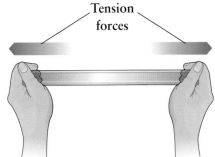

STRETCHING

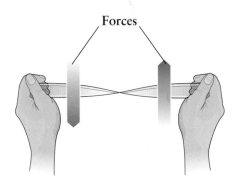

TWISTING

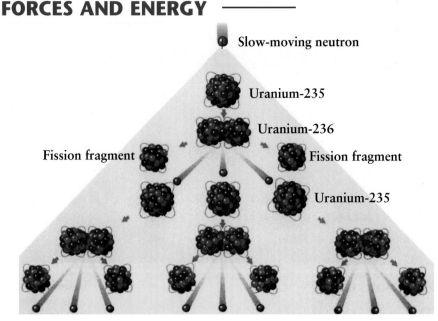

Slow-moving neutron

Uranium-235

Uranium-236

Fission fragment

Fission fragment

Uranium-235

Q What is gravity?

A Gravity is the force that pulls everything to Earth. Galileo showed that gravity makes all objects fall equally fast. When he dropped a light ball and a heavy ball from the Leaning Tower of Pisa (above), they hit the ground at the same instant.

Q What is an Archimedes' screw used for?

A The Archimedes' screw (below) was invented by Archimedes in ancient Greece. It is used for lifting water. One end of the screw is dipped into water. By turning the handle, the water is raised up inside the tube until it spills out of the top.

Q How is energy released inside a nuclear reactor?

A A slow-moving neutron is made to hit an atom of uranium-235 (above). It combines with the nucleus at the center of the atom, forming uranium-236. This splits into two particles called fission fragments, releasing a burst of energy and three more neutrons, which split more uranium atoms.

Q What forces act on an airplane in flight?

A Four forces act on an airplane. Its weight acts downward. The thrust of its engines pushes it forward. Lift created by its wings acts upward. Drag tries to slow it down. Thrust must overcome drag, and lift must overcome weight, if a plane is to fly.

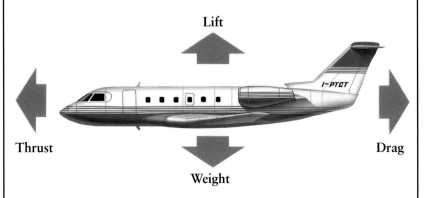

Lift

Thrust

Drag

Weight

Q How does a space rocket work?

A A rocket motor propels a rocket by burning fuel mixed with an oxidizer. The oxidizer contains oxygen, which is necessary for burning. The Ariane 5 rocket (below) burns hydrogen fuel with oxygen. The hot gas produced rushes out of the motor nozzles, forcing the rocket upward.

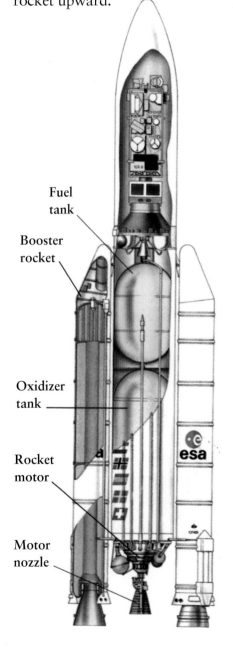

Fuel tank

Booster rocket

Oxidizer tank

Rocket motor

Motor nozzle

esa

Q What is a force?

A A force is something that changes an object's speed or direction. Forces always exist in pairs acting in opposite directions. When a rifle is fired (above left), the rifle kicks back as the bullet flies forward. A heavier football player running faster applies a greater force than a lighter, slower player (above right).

Q What is friction?

A Friction is a force that stops surfaces from sliding across each other easily. Sometimes friction is helpful. It allows our shoes to grip the ground. Without friction, walking would be impossible. But friction can also be a problem because it wears out the moving parts of machines.

Q How does a turbine work?

A A turbine (right) is a machine that uses gas or liquid to make a shaft turn. Water hitting the buckets of a Pelton wheel drives the buckets around and turns the shaft. Wind spins the blades of a wind turbine. Wind and water turbines often drive electricity generators.

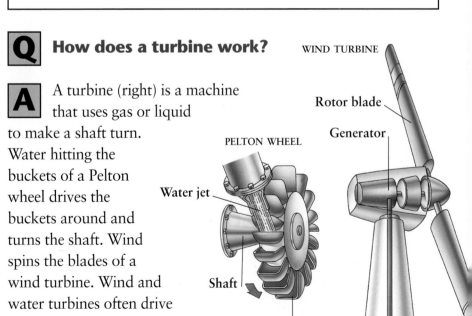

WIND TURBINE

Rotor blade

Generator

PELTON WHEEL

Water jet

Shaft

Buckets

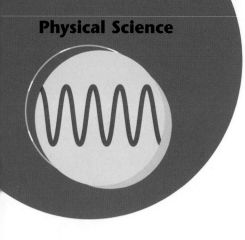

SOUND

Sound travels through air, water, and even solid materials such as metals. It travels in waves. When the waves reach a person's ears, the brain turns the vibrations into sounds that can be heard.

When something vibrates in air, the air molecules next to it are pushed together, then pulled apart. The molecules bump into the ones next to them, and they do the same. The vibrations spread farther and farther from the vibrating object. This is how sound travels, like a wave.

Sound cannot travel if there are no molecules to vibrate. So it will not move through a vacuum. It travels faster through a solid than it does through a liquid, and faster through a liquid than through a gas. In air at normal room temperature, sound travels at 768 miles per hour (1,236 kmh). Through steel, it moves much faster—at 12,950 miles per hour (20,845 kmh).

Volume

Sounds may be loud or soft. When someone rings a large church bell, it sounds much louder than a

KEY FACTS

Unit of sound frequency: Hertz (Hz). This is the number of sound waves registered per second. 1,000 Hz is the same as 1 kilohertz, or kHz.

Unit of loudness: Decibel (dB)

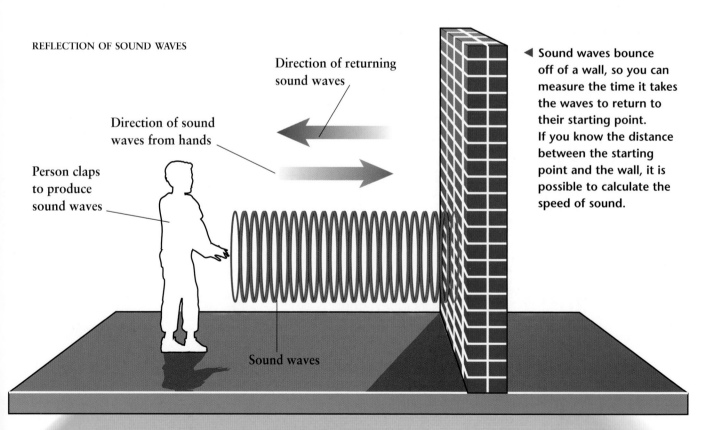

REFLECTION OF SOUND WAVES

Direction of returning sound waves

Direction of sound waves from hands

Person claps to produce sound waves

Sound waves

◄ Sound waves bounce off of a wall, so you can measure the time it takes the waves to return to their starting point. If you know the distance between the starting point and the wall, it is possible to calculate the speed of sound.

ULTRASOUND

Sounds with frequencies higher than 20,000 hertz (Hz) are called ultrasound. Humans cannot hear ultrasound, but animals such as dogs can. Bats (right) use ultrasound to locate their insect prey. They shout out high-pitched sound waves, then listen for the echoes. This is called echolocation.

squeaking mouse. Loudness, which is measured in decibels (dB), depends on the energy of the sound

▲ A woman's voice usually has a frequency between 165 and 255 Hz, while a man's is typically from 85 to 180 Hz. Bats make high-pitched sounds up to 100 kHz.

wave. The wave's energy depends on lots of things—for instance, how hard the church bell is struck.

Pitch

A squeaking mouse makes a high-pitched sound. A large bell being struck makes a low-pitched sound. Pitch is measured in hertz (Hz) and depends on the number of vibrations passing through the air each second. This is also called the frequency of the sound. Most people can hear sounds as high-pitched as 20,000 vibrations per second (20,000 Hz, or 20 kilohertz; kHz) and as low as 20 vibrations per second (20 Hz).

Echoes

If you shout into an empty room or a cave, you hear the echo of your own voice a few moments after you shout. Echoes are sound waves that have been reflected off walls and other objects.

Refraction

Sound waves can also be bent away from their original path if they pass from one substance to another—for example, from air to water. This is called refraction.

GENERAL INFORMATION

- The study of sound is called acoustics.

- A soft whisper 7 feet (2 m) away registers 30 decibels (dB). Every time the volume of the sound is doubled, the loudness increases by 10 dB. A person speaking very close is 70 dB. A jet aircraft taking off 200 feet (60 m) away is 120 dB.

- Units of sound frequency are named after the German scientist Heinrich Hertz (1857–1894).

- Sound bends around objects—as long as the objects are not very large. This is called the diffraction of sound.

SOUND

Direction of wave ▶

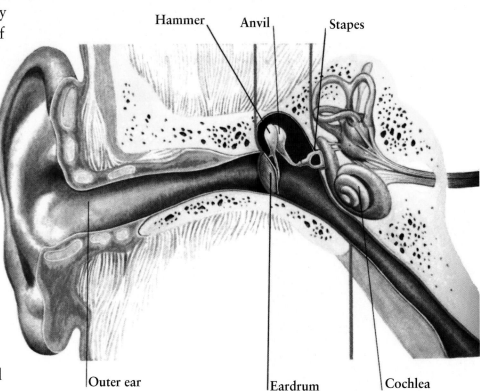

Rarefaction   Compression   Rarefaction

Q What is sound?

A Sound is a form of energy. Sound is made when something vibrates in air. The vibrations push against the surrounding air molecules, forming a sound wave. First, the air molecules are squeezed (this is called compression), then they are stretched (this is called rarefaction). It is easiest to think of sound waves moving in the same way as a wave of energy moves along a coiled spring if one end is repeatedly pushed and pulled (above).

Q How do we hear sounds?

A When sound waves reach us, the outer ear channels them inside the ear, where they make the eardrum vibrate. The vibrations are magnified twenty times by the hammer, anvil, and stapes bones, causing liquid to vibrate inside a tube called the cochlea (right). Nerves in the cochlea pass messages to the brain, enabling us to recognize the sound.

Hammer   Anvil   Stapes

Outer ear   Eardrum   Cochlea

Q How fast does sound travel?

A Sound travels through solids, liquids, and gases at different speeds. Its speed depends on the density of the material. It travels faster through dense materials like steel than through less dense materials, such as air (below).

Air 1,115 feet per second (340 m/s)

Water 4,920 feet per second (1,500 m/s)

Concrete 11,800 feet per second (3,600 m/s)

Steel 19,700 feet per second (6,000 m/s)

THE SPEED OF SOUND IN DIFFERENT MATERIALS

Q How is loudness measured?

A Loudness depends on the amount of energy carried by a sound wave. Loudness is measured in decibels (dB). Sounds louder than 120 dB can damage the ears. Sounds louder than 130 dB cause pain. Some animals, such as bats, make sounds that we cannot hear at all (below).

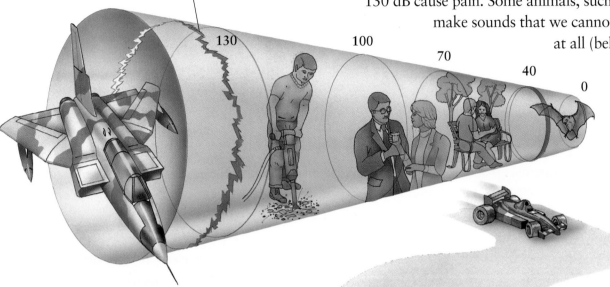

Decibels 140 Pain threshold

130   100   70   40   0

Q Why does the sound of a race car engine change as it drives past us?

A As the race car (right) approaches, the sound waves in front of it get squashed together. These short sound waves make the engine's noise sound high-pitched. As the car moves past, the sound waves become stretched out behind it. The longer waves make the engine's note sound lower.

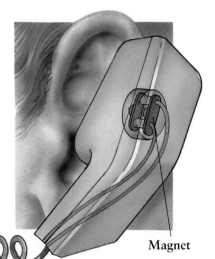

Q How does sound travel along telephone wires?

A A microphone in the mouthpiece (left) converts the sound pressure waves of the caller's voice into electrical signals. These flow along wires (below) to the telephone at the other end. The magnet in the earpiece (right) converts the signals back into sound pressure waves.

Microphone

Magnet

ELECTRICITY AND MAGNETISM

Electricity is the name given to anything that happens because of the presence or movement of charged particles. Magnetism is a force that draws some metals together or pushes them apart.

KEY FACTS

Unit of electrical current:
Ampere, or amp (A)
Unit of voltage: Volt (V)
Unit of magnetism: The strength of a magnetic field is measured in ampere-turns per meter (A/m)

Most people use electricity every day—to light homes, start cars, and operate computers and machinery.

Electricity comes from charged particles that are too small to see. Everything is made of atoms, and these are made up of even smaller particles called neutrons, protons, and electrons. Protons contain a small positive electrical charge, and electrons have a small negative charge. Usually, the number of protons and the number of electrons inside an atom are the same. The charges balance. If atoms lose some of their electrons, they become positively charged. If they gain electrons, they develop a negative charge.

Static Electricity

Particles with a positive charge attract those with a negative charge. If you rub a plastic ruler with a cloth, some of the electrons on the atoms from the ruler will rub off onto the cloth. The ruler will gain a positive charge and the cloth a negative charge. The cloth and the ruler will attract each other and stick together for a few seconds. This is static electricity.

Water heater:
3 units

Light bulb:
0.1 unit

Heater:
1 unit

Electric kettle:
2 units

Toaster:
1 unit

Iron: 1 unit

Sewing machine: 0.5 unit

Radio:
0.1 unit

Refrigerator:
0.2 unit

Cooking for 2 people: 2 units per day

Vacuum cleaner:
0.2 unit

TV set:
0.15 unit

Shower:
1 unit

◄ The diagram shows the number of units of electrical energy typically used by household appliances in one hour. Information such as this can help people reduce their energy usage.

GENERAL INFORMATION

- American inventor Thomas Edison (1847–1931) built the world's first electrical power plant in 1882.
- Earth has its own magnetic field. It is this that directs the needle on a compass.
- Magnets were once made from iron or nickel. The strongest magnets are now made from metals such as cobalt.

◀ Modern electromagnets are strong enough to lift loads of scrap metal.

Electrical Current

In the nineteenth century, scientists managed to get electrons to flow along wires. This flow is called electric current, and it works by electrical conduction. It allowed the use of many types of electrical machinery that used current generated in power plants.

CONDUCTORS AND INSULATORS

Some materials are better at conducting electrical current than others. They are called conductors. Metals are good conductors. Plastics, rubber, glass, and wood are poor conductors. They are called insulators. Plastic insulation is placed around wires to keep the charge from escaping.

Magnetism

Magnetism is the force that holds a magnet to a refrigerator and works a compass. Magnetism and electricity work together to make a force called electromagnetism.

Every electrical current creates its own magnetic field. And every magnet can create an electrical current. Electricity can be used to make very powerful magnets called electromagnets.

Compass needle (red) points in direction of magnetic field

Compass needle points in direction of magnetic field

Lines of magnetic field

Lines of magnetic field

N

S

North pole

South pole

▲ The area influenced by a magnet is called its magnetic field. The south pole on a compass points to the magnet's north pole and vice versa.

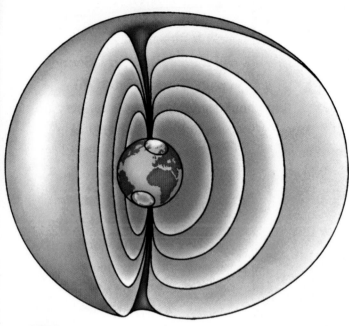

Q What is a magnetic field?

A A magnetic field is a region of forces that exists around a magnet. The field can be drawn as a series of curved lines, called lines of force, that join the magnet's north and south poles. The Earth behaves like a magnet. Its magnetic field (above), caused by electric currents inside the liquid part of its core, stretches thousands of miles into space.

Q How are magnets made?

A An iron bar contains molecular magnets pointing in all directions. If the bar is placed inside a coil carrying an electric current, the molecular magnets line up with the coil's magnetic field. The bar has now become a magnet (right).

Q How do electric vehicles work?

A An electric car (right) works by using electricity stored in batteries to power an electric motor connected to the car's wheels. Electric trains are supplied with electricity from wires above the track or a third rail beside the track. These power electric motors that turn the wheels.

Power plant

Transmission tower

Transformer

Q How do we get electricity?

A Electricity made at power plants (right) is distributed along cables at a very high voltage. The cables cross the countryside, strung between tall transmission towers. Electricity is distributed to towns by underground cables. Before it can be used, its voltage must be reduced by a transformer. The final voltage varies from country to country.

Q How do electric motors work?

A An electric motor is made of a coil of wire inside a magnet. The coil is free to turn. When an electric current flows through the coil, it magnetizes the coil. This magnetic field pushes against the magnetic field produced by the surrounding magnet, and this makes the coil spin.

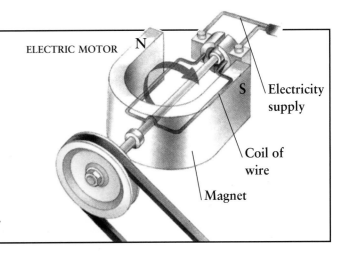

ELECTRIC MOTOR

N

S

Electricity supply

Coil of wire

Magnet

Q How does a doorbell work?

A When the doorbell push button (below) is pressed, the coil becomes magnetized. The iron rod shoots out of the coil and strikes the short chime. When the button is released, the rod swings back into the coil and hits the long chime.

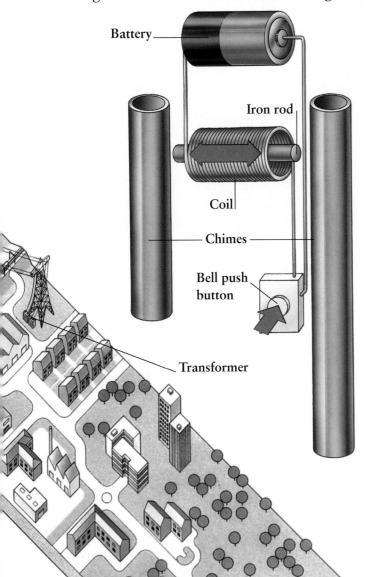

Battery

Iron rod

Coil

Chimes

Bell push button

Transformer

Q What is inside a battery?

A Cars and trucks use a type of battery called an accumulator (below). It contains flat plates of lead and lead oxide dipped in sulfuric acid. When the battery is connected to a circuit, a chemical reaction between the plates and the acid makes an electric current flow around the circuit. An accumulator is recharged by passing an electric current through it.

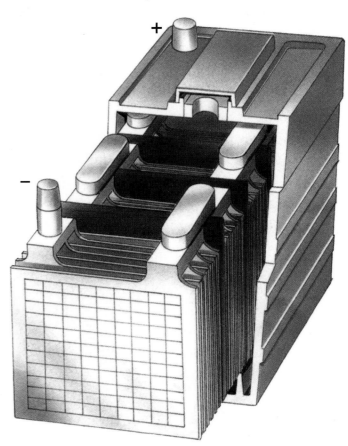

+

–

HEAT AND LIGHT

Heat and light are forms of energy. Heat is produced by the movement of the tiny particles that make up all matter. Light is made up of waves of electric and magnetic vibrations.

When heat energy is added to any material, its molecules vibrate faster and faster. This is true of the air around us on a summer day or the water in a boiling tea kettle. Heat naturally flows from hotter objects to cooler ones. Some of the energy of motion in the molecules in the hotter object is given to the molecules in the cooler one.

Making Heat

Heat can be produced in many ways. For instance, when an electrical current flows through a wire, the current makes the atoms of the wire move faster, and the wire gets hot. When two surfaces rub against each other at high speed, both surfaces will become hot because their molecules are vibrating faster. This is called friction. When sunshine beats down

▲ This furnace for making glass is giving off light and heat energy.

► When an object is cool, its molecules vibrate slowly. As it is heated, they vibrate more and more.

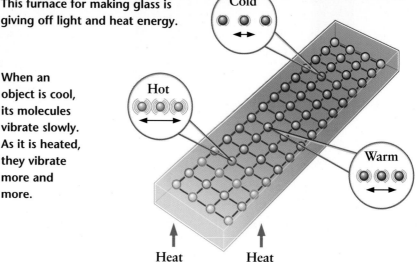

on a road, the infrared radiation within the sunlight excites the road's molecules. They vibrate faster and get hot.

Light

The main source of light is the sun. During the day, we see objects because they reflect sunlight into our eyes. Light is made up of moving waves of electric and magnetic energy. Light travels at 186,000 miles (300,000 km) per second. Scientists think that nothing travels faster than light.

Visible light cannot travel through everything. Nonvisible wavelengths, such as X-rays, can pass through more substances.

Refraction and Reflection

When light waves travel from one material to another, they bend, or

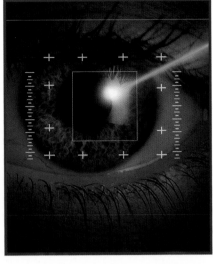

▲ A laser focuses light in a very narrow beam, producing heat. This can be used to cut through soft tissues in eye surgery.

refract. This is what happens when you hold a rod in water. The part of the rod above the water appears to be at an angle different from the part below the surface. Different substances bend light rays by different amounts. Light

GENERAL INFORMATION

- Heat is not the same as temperature.
- "Temperature" is the word used to describe how hot or cold something is. The temperature of something is not the same as how much heat it contains.
- The coldest temperature possible is called absolute zero. It is 0 kelvin (K), or −459.67°F (−273.15°C). No one knows what the hottest temperature is.
- Nearly every material gets bigger, or expands, when it heats up, and it gets smaller, or contracts, when it cools down.

waves cannot travel through a mirror, but they reflect off the silvery surface behind the glass, so you see a reversed image of yourself.

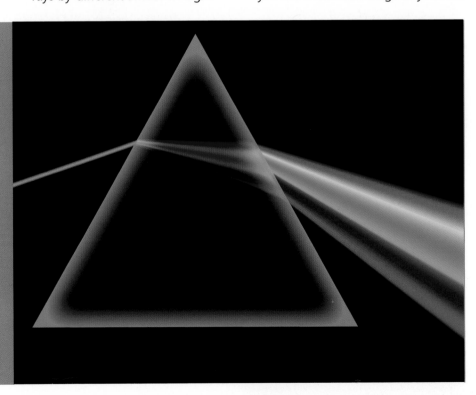

VISIBLE LIGHT SPECTRUM

When sunlight passes through a special block of glass called a prism (right), it splits into different colors, called a spectrum. We see the rainbow colors of the visible spectrum: red, orange, yellow, green, blue, indigo, and violet. Our eyes cannot see light of higher or lower wavelengths. Rays that are just longer than red light are called infrared and are felt as heat. Rays that are just shorter than violet light are called ultraviolet.

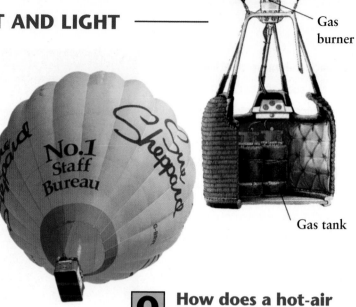

Gas burner

Gas tank

Q What is light?

A Light is a form of energy. It is composed of waves of electric and magnetic vibrations that our eyes can detect. The different colors (below) are produced by light waves of different lengths. We are unable to see waves shorter than blue light and longer than red.

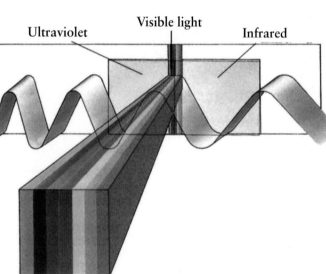

Ultraviolet   Visible light   Infrared

Q How does a hot-air balloon rise?

A A gas burner supplied with gas from tanks in the balloon's basket (above) heats the air inside the balloon. As the air warms up, it expands. The thinner air inside the balloon is lighter than the surrounding air, so the balloon floats upward.

Q How does a laser work?

A Light is normally composed of different wavelengths (colors) mixed at random. A laser produces an intense beam of high-energy light in which all the light is of the same wavelength. The process is started by an electric current or a flash of light from a flash tube, which causes a gas or ruby rod (below) to send out the laser beam.

Laser beam

Mirror

Ruby rod

Flash tube

Mirror

Q How fast does light travel?

A The speed of light is 186,000 miles per second (300,000 kms), faster than anything else in the universe. Light takes 8.5 minutes to travel from the sun (below) to Earth. Viewing distant objects allows us to look back in time. When we look at a remote galaxy, we see it as it was when light left it.

What are thermals?

A Birds can often be seen gliding in tight circles, being carried upward by rising columns of air called thermals (right). Ground heated by the sun warms the air above it. The warm air rises, sucking cool air in below it. That, too, is warmed and rises up. Glider pilots use thermals. They circle and climb inside one thermal, then glide to the next (below).

Bird's flight path

Thermal

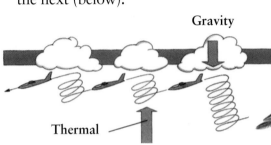

Gravity

Thermal

Q **How does a fluorescent tube work?**

A A hot wire inside the tube sends out particles called electrons, which scrash into atoms of mercury gas. The mercury atoms give out invisible ultraviolet radiation. The white phosphor coating inside the tube (below) changes this into bright visible light.

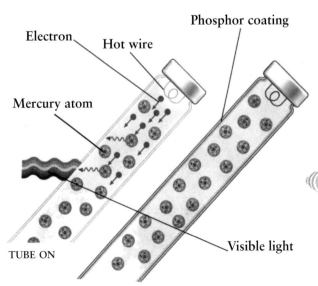

Phosphor coating

Electron   Hot wire

Mercury atom

TUBE ON

Visible light

TUBE OFF

Q **How does heat move along a metal bar?**

A When something is heated, its atoms vibrate. If one end of a metal bar is heated, the atoms at that end vibrate more than the atoms at the cold end. The vibration spreads along the bar from atom to atom. The spread of heat in this way is called conduction. Metals are good conductors of heat.

Cold

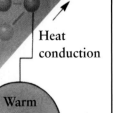

Hot

Heat conduction

Warm

GLOSSARY

chemical reaction A process that involves rearranging the molecules in a substance.

composite A thing that is made up of several parts.

compound Something that is made up of two or more elements in fixed proportions.

conductor A material that transmits electricity, heat, or sound.

element One of over one hundred substances that cannot be broken down.

energy A property of matter and radiation that makes things happen. Types of energy include heat, light, sound, mechanical, electrical, chemical, and nuclear.

force An influence that works on something to change the way it moves.

frequency The rate at which sound, radio, or light waves move over time.

gravity The force that attracts a physical object to the center of the Earth or toward another physical body with mass.

kinetic energy A type of energy that a body has due to its being in motion.

laser A machine that emits an intense beam of light, used for cutting and drilling.

magnetic field The area around something that has a magnetic charge.

material The matter from which a physical object is made.

organic Something that is made up of or related to living matter; a substance containing carbon. It also refers to a method of farming that does not use chemical fertilizers or pesticides.

periodic table A table that lists chemical elements by their number of protons.

recycling Converting a used material, such as a newspaper or a glass jar, into something new. Many household and industrial materials can be recycled.

refraction The bending of something, such as light, sound, or radio waves, when it hits an object.

state of matter A form that matter takes on. For instance, water exists as a liquid, a solid (ice), and a gas (steam).

thermal An upward current of warm air used by birds, airborne gliders, and hot-air balloons, for example.

ultrasound A band of sound above the range that human ears can hear. Ultrasound is used in medical imagery—for instance, to see the fetus inside of a pregnant woman.

visible light spectrum A band of colors that can be seen with the naked eye—violet, indigo, blue, green, yellow, orange, and red—as in a rainbow.

FURTHER READING

Books

Challoner, Jack, and Maggie Hewson. *Hands-On Science: Sound and Light*. New York: Kingfisher, 2013.

Coelho, Alexa, and Simon Quellen Field. *Why Is Milk White?: & 200 Other Curious Chemistry Questions*. Chicago: Chicago Review Press, 2013.

Hawkins, Jay. *Material World: The Science of Matter*. Big Bang Science Experiments. New York: Windmill Books, 2013.

Parker, Steve. *DK Eyewitness Books: Electricity*. New York: DK Children, 2013.

TIME For Kids Magazine editors. *TIME for Kids: Super Science Book*. New York: Time for Kids, 2009.

Websites

ACS's Adventures in Chemistry
www.acs.org/content/acs/en/education/whatischemistry/adventures-in-chemistry
Discover how chemical reactions work, and try experiments from this cool and colorful site. From the Secret Science of Stuff, to Games and Science ABCs, you'll learn about everyday processes the fun way.

Energy Kids
www.eia.gov/kids
Learn all about energy, from the different sources of energy to the laws of sound and light. Also, find out ways in which you can conserve fuel energy. With games and activities, such as riddles, puzzles, and science fair experiments, that will make learning about physical science exciting.

Exploratorium
www.exploratorium.edu/explore
Check out the latest in light, sound, matter, energy, color, chemistry, and more at this amazing site from San Francisco's hands-on science museum. With videos, photos, articles, and experiments.

Publisher's note to educators and parents: Our editors have carefully reviewed these websites to ensure that they are suitable for students. Many websites change frequently, however, and we cannot guarantee that a site's future contents will continue to meet our high standards of quality and educational value. Be advised that students should be closely supervised whenever they access the Internet.

INDEX